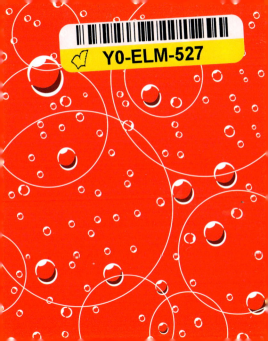

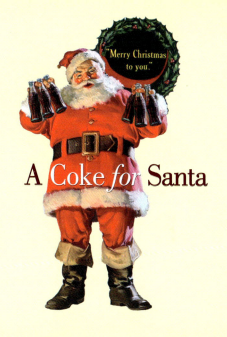

A Coke

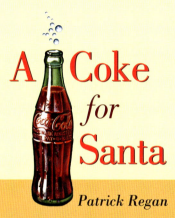

for

Santa

Patrick Regan

Andrews McMeel
Publishing

Kansas City

Coke™ publications are produced for
The Coca-Cola Company, owner of
the trademarks COCA-COLA, COKE,
the design of the contour bottle,
the design of the COCA-COLA
Santa and the Red Disk Icon,
and for Coca-Cola Ltd. owner
of the trademarks in Canada,
by Lionheart Books.

ISBN: 0-7407-2258-1

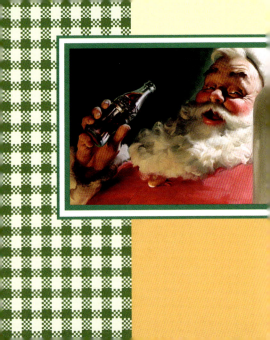

There's a *magic night* each year when a man of *great renown . . .*

"Wherever I go"

Spreads *holiday excitement* to kids the whole world round.

His itinerary's legendary—
He stops at *every home . . .*

From *Kathmandu to Timbuktu . . .* from Senegal to Nome.

DRINK
Coca-Cola

Greetings

And if you sent *a letter* and *behaved* as you were told . . .

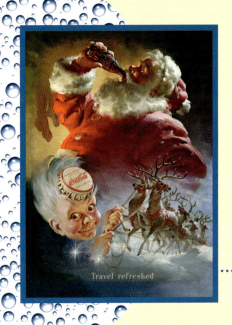

Travel refreshed

He's sure to steer his sleigh *your way,* through winter's *snow and cold.*

Drink Coca-Cola

But here's a *little secret* not everybody knows...

"Whereve

There's a *special treat*
that Santa likes—
no matter where he goes.

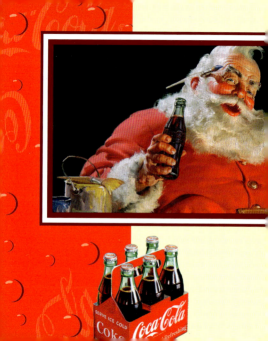

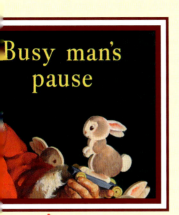

Busy man's
pause

And even though the
night is short
and he's *a busy man . . .*

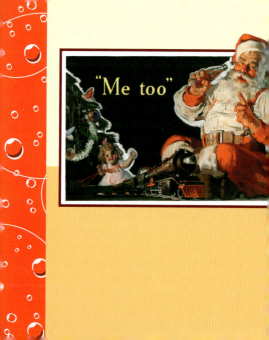

Drink Coca-Cola

The pause
that refreshes

Y ou're sure to cause
St. Nick to pause
by following *this plan . . .*

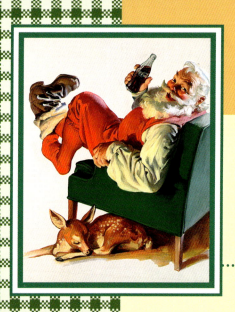

See Santa's *not too different* from most *other folks* you know...

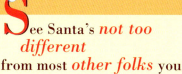

Have a Coke

ICE COLD

PAUSE-REFRESH

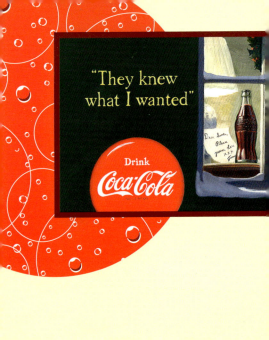

He needs *refreshment* now and then to keep him *on the go.*

So leave *a snack* for Santa and *a Coke* for him to drink . . .

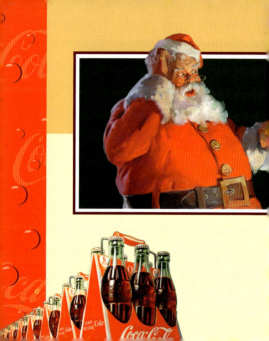

And *don't forget* to leave a note *to tell him* what you think.

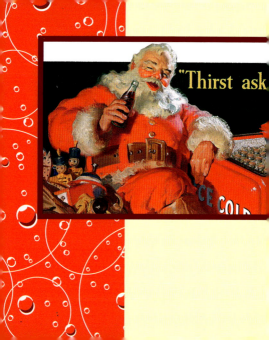

"...othing more"

DRINK
Coca-Cola
ICE COLD

DRINK
Coca-Cola

And while the
jolly one enjoys
a treat cold and *delicious* . . .

Perhaps you'll get a
peek at him . . .
If you're quite
surreptitious.

So before you *shuffle off* to bed this snowy Christmas Eve,

"Have a Coke"

Coca-Cola

Pause...
Go refreshed

Coca-Cola

R emember, kids, 'tis
better still
to give than to receive.

Now